This book belongs to:

· ·

From:

· ·

Date:

· · · · · · · · · · · · · · · · ·

77 Memory Verses Every Kid Should Know

Copyright © 2019 by Christian Art Kids,
an imprint of Christian Art Publishers,
PO Box 1599, Vereeniging, 1930, RSA

© 2019
First edition 2019

Designed by Christian Art Kids

Images used under license from Shutterstock.com

Printed in China

ISBN 978-1-4321-3077-0

19 20 21 22 23 24 25 26 27 28 – 12 11 10 9 8 7 6 5 4 3

Printed in Shenzhen, China
November 2019
Print Run: 100644

77
MEMORY VERSES
EVERY KID
SHOULD KNOW

christian art kids

Read it ...

> Your word is a lamp for my feet,
> a light on my path.
>
> Psalm 119:105

Write it

Read it ...

May the God of hope
fill you with all joy
and peace in believing.

Romans 15:13

Write it

Read it ...

I can do everything
through Christ,
who gives me strength.

Philippians 4:13

Write it

Color it!

I CAN DO

everything

through Christ

WHO GIVES ME

strength.

PHILIPPIANS
4:13

Read it ...

God so loved the world that He gave His one and only Son, that whoever believes in Him shall not perish but have eternal life.

John 3:16

Write it

Color it!

GOD SO LOVED THE world that He gave His one and only Son, that whoever believes in HiM shall not perish but have eternal LIFE.

John 3:16

Read it ...

> Jesus said, "I am the way,
> and the truth, and the life.
> No one comes to the Father
> except through Me."
>
> John 14:6

Write it

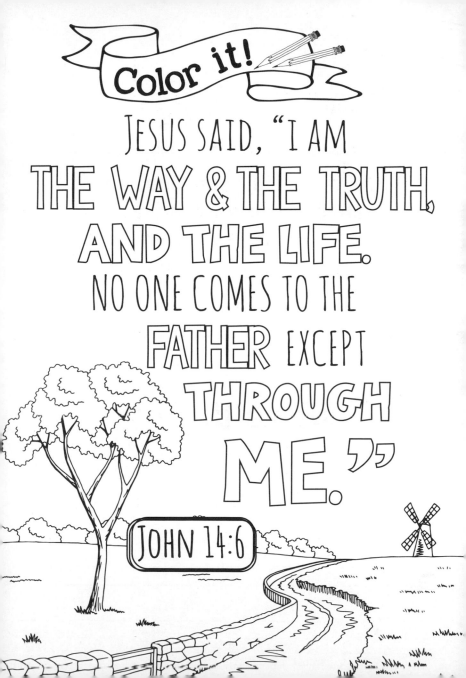

Read it ...

Love the Lord your God with all your heart and with all your soul and with all your mind and with all your strength.

Mark 12:30

Write it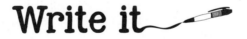

Color it!

Love THE LORD your God WITH ALL YOUR heart, soul, MIND AND strength.

Mark 12:30

Read it ...

> "Do to others
> as you would have
> them do to you."
>
> Luke 6:31

Write it

_____

_____

_____

_____

_____

Color it!

DO TO OTHERS

As you would **HAVE THEM**

DO TO YOU.

LUKE 6:31

Read it ...

> "Love your neighbor
> as yourself."
>
> Matthew 22:39

Write it

_____

_____

_____

_____

_____

Read it ...

Children, obey your parents
in all things, for this
is well pleasing to the Lord.

Colossians 3:20

Write it

Color it!

CHILDREN, OBEY YOUR PARENTS in all THINGS, FOR THIS IS well pleasing TO THE LORD.

Colossians 3:20

Read it ...

Trust in the LORD with all your heart and lean not on your own understanding; in all your ways submit to Him, and He will make your paths straight.

Proverbs 3:5-6

Write it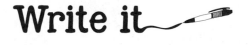

Color it!

Trust in the Lord with ALL YOUR HEART

and lean not on your own understanding;

IN ALL YOUR WAYS

SUBMIT TO HIM,

AND HE WILL MAKE

YOUR PATHS STRAIGHT.

PROVERBS 3:5-6

Read it ...

> "I know the plans I have for you," says the LORD. "They are plans for good and not for disaster, to give you a future and a hope."
>
> Jeremiah 29:11

Write it

Read it ...

> The faithful love
> of the LORD never ends!
> His mercies never cease.
>
> Lamentations 3:22

Write it

Read it ...

> Give all your worries and cares
> to God, for He cares about you.
>
> 1 Peter 5:7

Write it

Read it ...

> Give thanks to the LORD,
> for He is good.
> His love endures forever.
>
> Psalm 136:1

Write it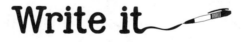

Read it ...

Whether you eat or drink,
or whatever you do, do all to
the glory of God.

1 Corinthians 10:31

Write it

Read it ...

> "Be strong and courageous. Do not be afraid; do not be discouraged, for the LORD your God will be with you wherever you go."
>
> Joshua 1:9

Write it

_____

_____

_____

_____

_____

Color it!

Be STRONG and courageous. Do not be afraid; do not be discouraged, for the LORD YOUR GOD WILL BE WITH YOU wherever you go.

JOSHUA 1:9

Read it ...

> Rejoice always, pray without ceasing, in everything give thanks; for this is the will of God in Christ Jesus for you.
>
> 1 Thessalonians 5:16–18

Write it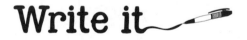

Read it ...

Every word of God is flawless;
He is a shield to those
who take refuge in Him.

Proverbs 30:5

Write it

19

Read it ...

> The LORD is my shepherd;
> I shall not want.
>
> Psalm 23:1

Write it

THE LORD is my shepherd; I SHALL NOT WANT.

Psalm 23:1

Read it ...

> The LORD is good to all;
> He has compassion on all
> He has made.
>
> Psalm 145:9

Write it

Color it!

THE LORD is good TO ALL; HE HAS COMPASSION ON ALL HE HAS made.

PSALM 145:9

Read it ...

> We know that in all things God works for the good of those who love Him, who have been called according to His purpose.
>
> Romans 8:28

Write it

_____

_____

_____

_____

Color it!

We know THAT IN all things GOD works FOR THE good OF THOSE WHO love HIM, WHO HAVE BEEN CALLED ACCORDING TO HIS PURPOSE.

Romans 8:28

Read it ...

> Three things will last forever –
> faith, hope, and love –
> and the greatest
> of these is love.
>
> 1 Corinthians 13:13

Write it

Color it!

Three things will last forever –

faith, hope, and love –

& the greatest of these is love.

1 CORINTHIANS 13:13

Read it ...

Delight yourself in the LORD,
and He will give you the desires
of your heart.

Psalm 37:4

Write it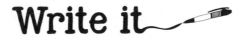

_____

_____

_____

_____

_____

Color it!

DELIGHT yourself in the LORD, and He will GIVE YOU the DESIRES of your heart. Psalm 37:4

Read it ...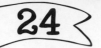

> The fruit of the Spirit is love, joy, peace, patience, kindness, goodness, faithfulness, gentleness, self-control.
>
> Galatians 5:22-23

Write it

Color it!

The fruit of the Spirit is

LOVE, JOY,

PEACE,

PATIENCE,

KINDNESS, GOODNESS,

FAITHFULNESS, GENTLENESS,

SELF-CONTROL.

Galatians 5:22–23

Read it ...

Let us run with endurance
the race that is set before us,
looking to Jesus, the founder
and perfecter of our faith.

Hebrews 12:1-2

Write it

Let us run with ENDURANCE the race that is set before us, looking to Jesus, the founder & PERFECTER of our faith.

Hebrews 12:1-2

Read it ...

> Know that the LORD, He is God!
> It is He who made us,
> and we are His; we are His people,
> and the sheep of His pasture.
>
> Psalm 100:3

Write it

Color it!

KNOW THAT THE LORD,
HE IS GOD!
IT IS HE WHO *made us,*
AND WE ARE His;
WE ARE HIS PEOPLE,
AND THE SHEEP
OF HIS PASTURE.

Psalm 100:3

Read it ...

The LORD your God is with you,
the Mighty Warrior who saves.

Zephaniah 3:17

Write it

Color it!

THE LORD YOUR GOD IS with you, the MIGHTY WARRIOR WHO SAVES.

ZEPHANIAH 3:17

Read it ...

> "Let your light shine
> before others, that they may see
> your good deeds and glorify your
> Father in heaven."
>
> Matthew 5:16

Write it

Read it ...

Commit your actions to the LORD,
and your plans will succeed.

Proverbs 16:3

Write it

Read it ...

"Peace I leave with you;
My peace I give you."

John 14:27

Write it

Read it ...

Jesus declared,
"I am the bread of life.
Whoever comes to Me will never
go hungry, and whoever believes
in Me will never be thirsty."

John 6:35

Write it

Color it!

JESUS DECLARED, "I AM THE *bread of Life.* WHOEVER *comes to Me* WILL NEVER GO HUNGRY, AND WHOEVER *believes* in Me WILL NEVER BE *thirsty.*"

John 6:35

Read it ...

Create in me a clean heart, O God, and renew a right spirit within me.

Psalm 51:10

Write it

Read it ...

God has not given us
a spirit of fear,
but of power and of love
and of a sound mind.

2 Timothy 1:7

Write it

Read it ...

Come near to God and
He will come near to you.

James 4:8

Write it

Read it ...

Jesus called out, "Come, follow Me,
and I will show you
how to fish for people!"

Mark 1:17

Write it

Read it ...

The LORD is good,
a refuge in times of trouble.
He cares for those
who trust in Him.

Nahum 1:7

Write it

Read it ...

> We are God's handiwork,
> created in Christ Jesus
> to do good works.
>
> Ephesians 2:10

Write it

Read it ...

"I am the Alpha and the Omega –
the beginning and the end,"
says the Lord God.

Revelation 1:8

Write it

Read it ...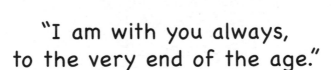

"I am with you always,
to the very end of the age."

Matthew 28:20

Write it

Color it!

I am with you always, to the very end of the age.

Matthew 28:20

Read it ...

If God is for us,
who can be against us?

Romans 8:31

Write it

Color it!

If God is for US, WHO CAN BE AGAINST US?

Romans 8:31

Read it ...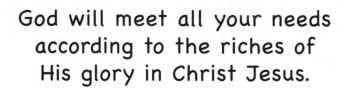

God will meet all your needs
according to the riches of
His glory in Christ Jesus.

Philippians 4:19

Write it

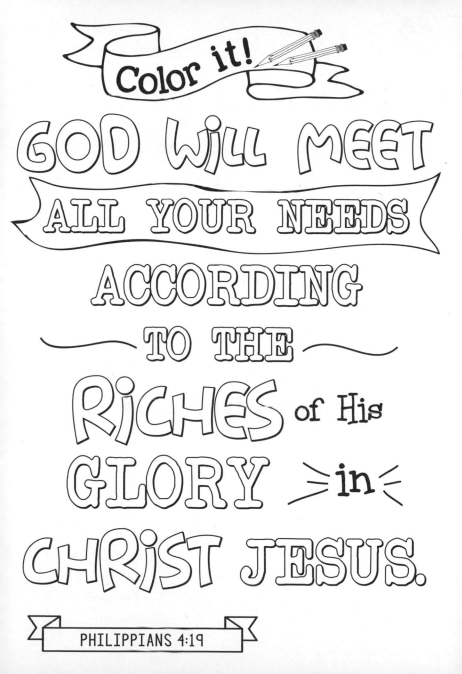

Color it!

GOD WILL MEET ALL YOUR NEEDS ACCORDING TO THE RICHES of His GLORY in CHRIST JESUS.

PHILIPPIANS 4:19

Read it ...

The LORD always
keeps His promises;
He is gracious
in all He does.

Psalm 145:13

Write it

Color it!

THE LORD always keeps His PROMISES; He is gracious in all He DOES.

Psalm 145:13

Read it ...

Rejoice in the Lord always.
I will say it again: Rejoice!

Philippians 4:4

Write it

Read it ...

God has said,
"Never will I leave you;
never will I forsake you."

Hebrews 13:5

Write it

Read it ...

> "Be still, and know
> that I am God."
>
> Psalm 46:10

Write it

Read it ...

"My grace is all you need.
My power works best in weakness."

2 Corinthians 12:9

Write it

Read it ...

Jesus said, "Come to Me, all of you who are weary and carry heavy burdens, and I will give you rest."

Matthew 11:28

Write it

Read it ...

Those who hope in the LORD
will renew their strength.
They will soar on wings like eagles;
they will run and not grow weary,
they will walk and not be faint.

Isaiah 40:31

Write it

Read it ...

Don't worry about anything;
instead, pray about everything.
Tell God what you need, and thank
Him for all He has done.

Philippians 4:6

Write it

Color it!

Don't worry about ANYTHING; INSTEAD, pray about everything. TELL GOD what you need & THANK HIM FOR ALL HE HAS DONE. Philippians 4:6

50

Read it ...

Fix your thoughts on what is true,
and honorable, and right, and pure,
and lovely, and admirable.
Think about things that are
excellent and worthy of praise.

Philippians 4:8

Write it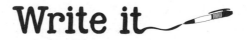

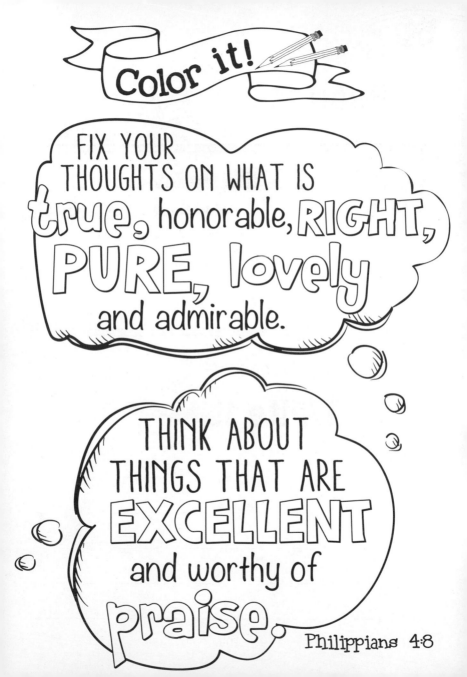

51

Read it ...

Don't copy the behavior and customs of this world, but let God transform you into a new person by changing the way you think.

Romans 12:2

Write it

_____

_____

_____

_____

_____

Color it!

Don't copy the behavior and CUSTOMS of this WORLD, BUT LET GOD transform you into a NEW PERSON by changing THE WAY YOU THINK. ROMANS 12:2

Read it ...

God showed His great love for us by sending Christ to die for us while we were still sinners.

Romans 5:8

Write it

Color it!

GOD SHOWED HIS GREAT *love* FOR US BY SENDING CHRIST TO DIE FOR US WHILE WE WERE STILL SINNERS.

ROMANS 5:8

Read it ...

Faith is confidence in what we hope for and assurance about what we do not see.

Hebrews 11:1

Write it

54

Read it ...

> From His abundance we have all received one gracious blessing after another.
>
> John 1:16

Write it

Read it ...

> Give your burdens to the LORD,
> and He will take care of you.
>
> Psalm 55:22

Write it

Read it ...

God is our God for ever and ever;
He will be our guide
even to the end.

Psalm 48:14

Write it

Color it!

GOD IS OUR GOD for ever and ever; HE WILL be our guide EVEN TO the end.

PSALM 48:14

Read it ...

"Ask and it will be given to you; seek and you will find; knock and the door will be opened to you."

Matthew 7:7

Write it

Color it!

ASK AND IT WILL BE GIVEN TO YOU; SEEK & YOU WILL FIND; KNOCK AND THE DOOR WILL BE OPENED TO YOU.

MATTHEW 7:7

Read it ...

"In this world you will have
trouble. But take heart!
I have overcome the world."

John 16:33

Write it

Color it!

In this **WORLD** you will have trouble.

BUT TAKE HEART!

I have

OVERCOME

THE WORLD.

JOHN 16:33

Read it ...

The heavens declare
the glory of God;
the skies proclaim
the work of His hands.

Psalm 19:1

Write it

Color it!

THE heavens declare the glory OF GOD; THE skies proclaim the work OF HIS HANDS.

Psalm 19:1

Read it ...

Jesus Christ is the same yesterday, today, and forever.

Hebrews 13:8

Write it

Color it!

JESUS CHRIST IS THE SAME yesterday, TODAY, and FOREVER.

Hebrews 13:8

Read it ...

The prayer of a righteous person is powerful and effective.

James 5:16

Write it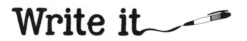

Read it ...

> The LORD is compassionate and merciful, slow to get angry and filled with unfailing love.
>
> Psalm 103:8

Write it

Color it!

THE LORD IS COMPASSIONATE and merciful, SLOW TO GET ANGRY AND filled with UNFAILING LOVE.

PSALM 103:8

Read it ...

Love is patient, love is kind.
It does not envy, it does not boast,
it is not proud.

1 Corinthians 13:4

Write it

Color it!

LOVE IS PATIENT, LOVE IS KIND. IT DOES NOT ENVY, IT DOES NOT BOAST, IT IS NOT PROUD.

1 Corinthians 13:4

Read it ...

Jesus said, "I am the light
of the world. Whoever follows Me
will never walk in darkness,
but will have the light of life."

John 8:12

Write it

Read it ...

Anyone who belongs to Christ
has become a new person.
The old life is gone;
a new life has begun!

2 Corinthians 5:17

Write it

Color it!

Anyone WHO BELONGS TO Christ HAS BECOME A new person. THE OLD LIFE IS GONE; a new life has begun!

2 Corinthians 5:17

Read it ...

> "Do not fear, for I have redeemed you; I have summoned you by name; you are Mine."
>
> Isaiah 43:1

Write it

Color it!

DO NOT FEAR,
for I have redeemed
YOU; I have
SUMMONED YOU
BY NAME,
YOU ARE
MINE.

ISAIAH 43:1

Read it ...

"Where your treasure is,
there your heart will be also."

Matthew 6:21

Write it

Color it!

Where YOUR treasure IS,

THERE YOUR heart WILL BE also.

Matthew 6:21

Read it ...

Let us love one another,
for love comes from God.

1 John 4:7

Write it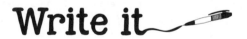

Read it ...

God is love.

1 John 4:8

Write it

Color it!

GOD is LOVE.

1 John 4:8

Read it ...

Kind words are like honey –
sweet to the soul
and healthy for the body.

Proverbs 16:24

Write it

Read it ...

> God loves a cheerful giver.
>
> 2 Corinthians 9:7

Write it

_____

_____

_____

_____

_____

Read it ...

Work willingly at whatever you do,
as though you were working
for the Lord
rather than for people.

Colossians 3:23

Write it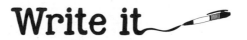

Read it ...

For the wages of sin is death,
but the free gift of God is
eternal life through
Christ Jesus our Lord.

Romans 6:23

Write it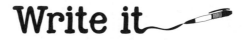

Color it!

FOR THE WAGES OF SIN
IS DEATH,
but the free
gift of God
IS ETERNAL LIFE
THROUGH
CHRIST JESUS
OUR LORD.

Romans 6:23

Read it ...

"Forgive,
and you will be forgiven."

Luke 6:37

Write it

Read it ...

The earth is the LORD's,
and everything in it.
The world and all its people
belong to Him.

Psalm 24:1

Write it

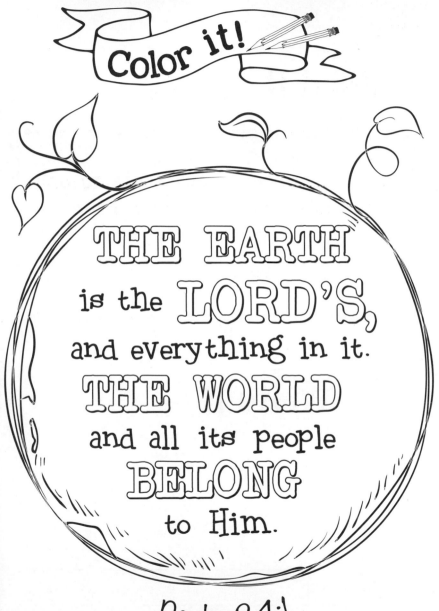

Color it!

THE EARTH is the LORD'S, and everything in it. THE WORLD and all its people BELONG to Him.

Psalm 24:1

76

Read it ...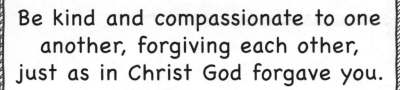

Be kind and compassionate to one another, forgiving each other, just as in Christ God forgave you.

Ephesians 4:32

Write it

_____

_____

_____

_____

_____

Color it!

BE KIND and compassionate TO ONE *another,* FORGIVING each other, just as in CHRIST GOD *forgave* you.

Ephesians 4:32

77

Read it ...

Do everything without
complaining and arguing.

Philippians 2:14

Write it

DO everything without complaining and arguing.

Philippians 2:14

Tick the Scripture verses you've memorized

1. Your word is a lamp for my feet, a light on my path. (Ps.119:105) ☐
2. May the God of hope fill you with all joy and peace in believing. (Rom. 15:13) ☐
3. I can do everything through Christ, who gives me strength. (Phil. 4:13) ☐
4. God so loved the world that He gave His one and only Son, that whoever believes in Him shall not perish but have eternal life. (John 3:16) ☐
5. Jesus said, "I am the way, and the truth, and the life. No one comes to the Father except through Me." (John 14:6) ☐
6. Love the Lord your God with all your heart and with all your soul and with all your mind and with all your strength. (Mark 12:30) ☐
7. "Do to others as you would have them do to you." (Luke 6:31) ☐
8. "Love your neighbor as yourself." (Matt. 22:39) ☐
9. Children, obey your parents in all things, for this is well pleasing to the Lord. (Col. 3:20) ☐
10. Trust in the LORD with all your heart and lean not on your own understanding; in all your ways submit to Him, and He will make your paths straight. (Prov. 3:5-6) ☐
11. "I know the plans I have for you," says the LORD. "They are plans for good and not for disaster, to give you a future and a hope." (Jer. 29:11) ☐
12. The faithful love of the LORD never ends! His mercies never cease. (Lam. 3:22) ☐
13. Give all your worries and cares to God, for He cares about you. (1 Pet. 5:7) ☐
14. Give thanks to the LORD, for He is good. His love endures forever. (Ps. 136:1) ☐
15. Whether you eat or drink, or whatever you do, do all to the glory of God. (1 Cor. 10:31) ☐
16. "Be strong and courageous. Do not be afraid; do not be discouraged, for the LORD your God will be with you wherever you go." (Josh. 1:9) ☐
17. Rejoice always, pray without ceasing, in everything give thanks; for this is the will of God in Christ Jesus for you. (1 Thess. 5:16-18) ☐
18. Every word of God is flawless; He is a shield to those who take refuge in Him. (Prov. 30:5) ☐
19. The LORD is my shepherd; I shall not want. (Ps. 23:1) ☐
20. The LORD is good to all; He has compassion on all He has made. (Ps. 145:9) ☐
21. We know that in all things God works for the good of those who love Him, who have been called according to His purpose. (Rom. 8:28) ☐
22. Three things will last forever – faith, hope, and love – and the greatest of these is love. (1 Cor. 13:13) ☐
23. Delight yourself in the LORD, and He will give you the desires of your heart. (Ps. 37:4) ☐
24. The fruit of the Spirit is love, joy, peace, patience, kindness, goodness, faithfulness, gentleness, self-control. (Gal. 5:22-23) ☐
25. Let us run with endurance the race that is set before us, looking to Jesus, the founder and perfecter of our faith. (Heb. 12:1-2) ☐

26. Know that the LORD, He is God! It is He who made us, and we are His; we are His people, and the sheep of His pasture. (Ps. 100:3) ☐
27. The LORD your God is with you, the Mighty Warrior who saves. (Zeph. 3:17) ☐
28. "Let your light shine before others, that they may see your good deeds and glorify your Father in heaven." (Matt. 5:16) ☐
29. Commit your actions to the LORD, and your plans will succeed. (Prov. 16:3) ☐
30. "Peace I leave with you; My peace I give you." (John 14:27) ☐
31. Jesus declared, "I am the bread of life. Whoever comes to Me will never go hungry, and whoever believes in Me will never be thirsty." (John 6:35) ☐
32. Create in me a clean heart, O God, and renew a right spirit within me. (Ps. 51:10) ☐
33. God has not given us a spirit of fear, but of power and of love and of a sound mind. (2 Tim. 1:7) ☐
34. Come near to God and He will come near to you. (James 4:8) ☐
35. Jesus called out, "Come, follow Me, and I will show you how to fish for people!" (Mark 1:17) ☐
36. The LORD is good, a refuge in times of trouble. He cares for those who trust in Him. (Nah. 1:7) ☐
37. We are God's handiwork, created in Christ Jesus to do good works. (Eph. 2:10) ☐
38. "I am the Alpha and the Omega – the beginning and the end," says the Lord God. (Rev. 1:8) ☐
39. "I am with you always, to the very end of the age." (Matt. 28:20) ☐
40. If God is for us, who can be against us? (Rom. 8:31) ☐
41. God will meet all your needs according to the riches of His glory in Christ Jesus. (Phil. 4:19) ☐
42. The Lord always keeps His promises; He is gracious in all He does. (Ps. 145:13) ☐
43. Rejoice in the Lord always. I will say it again: Rejoice! (Phil. 4:4) ☐
44. God has said, "Never will I leave you; never will I forsake you." (Heb. 13:5) ☐
45. "Be still, and know that I am God." (Ps. 46:10) ☐
46. "My grace is all you need. My power works best in weakness." (2 Cor. 12:9) ☐
47. Jesus said, "Come to Me, all of you who are weary and carry heavy burdens, and I will give you rest." (Matt. 11:28) ☐
48. Those who hope in the LORD will renew their strength. They will soar on wings like eagles; they will run and not grow weary, they will walk and not be faint. (Isa. 40:31) ☐
49. Don't worry about anything; instead, pray about everything. Tell God what you need, and thank Him for all He has done. (Phil. 4:6) ☐
50. Fix your thoughts on what is true, and honorable, and right, and pure, and lovely, and admirable. Think about things that are excellent and worthy of praise. (Phil. 4:8) ☐
51. Don't copy the behavior and customs of this world, but let God transform you into a new person by changing the way you think. (Rom. 12:2) ☐

52. God showed His great love for us by sending Christ to die for us while we were still sinners. (Rom. 5:8)

53. Faith is confidence in what we hope for and assurance about what we do not see. (Heb. 11:1)

54. From His abundance we have all received one gracious blessing after another. (John 1:16)

55. Give your burdens to the LORD, and He will take care of you. (Ps. 55:22)

56. God is our God for ever and ever; He will be our guide even to the end. (Ps. 48:14)

57. "Ask and it will be given to you; seek and you will find; knock and the door will be opened to you." (Matt. 7:7)

58. "In this world you will have trouble. But take heart! I have overcome the world." (John 16:33)

59. The heavens declare the glory of God; the skies proclaim the work of His hands. (Ps. 19:1)

60. Jesus Christ is the same yesterday, today, and forever. (Heb. 13:8)

61. The prayer of a righteous person is powerful and effective. (James 5:16)

62. The LORD is compassionate and merciful, slow to get angry and filled with unfailing love. (Ps. 103:8)

63. Love is patient, love is kind. It does not envy, it does not boast, it is not proud. (1 Cor. 13:4)

64. Jesus said, "I am the light of the world. Whoever follows Me will never walk in darkness, but will have the light of life." (John 8:12)

65. Anyone who belongs to Christ has become a new person. The old life is gone; a new life has begun! (2 Cor. 5:17)

66. "Do not fear, for I have redeemed you; I have summoned you by name; you are Mine." (Isa. 43:1)

67. "Where your treasure is, there your heart will be also." (Matt. 6:21)

68. Let us love one another, for love comes from God. (1 John 4:7)

69. God is love. (1 John 4:8)

70. Kind words are like honey – sweet to the soul and healthy for the body. (Prov. 16:24)

71. God loves a cheerful giver. (2 Cor. 9:7)

72. Work willingly at whatever you do, as though you were working for the Lord rather than for people. (Col. 3:23)

73. For the wages of sin is death, but the free gift of God is eternal life through Christ Jesus our Lord. (Rom. 6:23)

74. "Forgive, and you will be forgiven." (Luke 6:37)

75. The earth is the LORD's, and everything in it. The world and all its people belong to Him. (Ps. 24:1)

76. Be kind and compassionate to one another, forgiving each other, just as in Christ God forgave you. (Eph. 4:32)

77. Do everything without complaining and arguing. (Phil. 2:14)